Lerner SPORTS ROOKIE

I0878816

SOCCER MANIA

THE STORY OF THE WORLD CUP

Emma Carlson-Berne

Lerner Publications ◆ Minneapolis

To Abe

Statistics in this book are accurate through September 6, 2024.

Lerner Publications Company
An imprint of Lerner Publishing Group, Inc.
241 First Avenue North
Minneapolis, MN 55401 USA

For reading levels and more information, look up this title at www.lernerbooks.com.

Main body text set in Mikado. Typeface provided by HVD fonts.

Editor: Nicole Berglund **Designer:** Viet Chu **Photo Editor:** Nicole Berglund
Lerner team: Sue Marquis

Library of Congress Cataloging-in-Publication Data

Names: Berne, Emma Carlson, 1979–
Title: The story of the World Cup / Emma Carlson-Berne.
Description: Minneapolis, MN : Lerner Publications, [2026] | Series: Soccer mania (Lerner sports rookie) | Includes bibliographical references and index. | Audience: Ages 5–8 | Audience: Grades K–1 | Summary: "The best soccer teams compete in the World Cup every four years. Readers discover the World Cup and some of the teams and players that make it great"— Provided by publisher.
Identifiers: LCCN 2024038793 (print) | LCCN 2024038794 (ebook) | ISBN 9798765668405 (library binding) | ISBN 9798765683750 (paperback) | ISBN 9798765681213 (epub)
Subjects: LCSH: World Cup (Soccer)—Juvenile literature. | Soccer teams—Juvenile literature. | Soccer—History—Juvenile literature.
Classification: LCC GV943.49 .B47 2026 (print) | LCC GV943.49 (ebook) | DDC 796.334/66809—dc23/eng/20240826

LC record available at https://lccn.loc.gov/2024038793
LC ebook record available at https://lccn.loc.gov/2024038794

Manufactured in the United States of America
1-1011711-53808-1/29/2025

Table of Contents

Goal! 4

Glossary 24

Learn More 24

Index 24

Goal!

Argentina was facing England in the 1986 World Cup. Argentina player Diego Maradona shot and scored! His goal became known as the Goal of the Century.

ARG 1 ENG 0 09:13
JVC
Diego Maradona

The World Cup is a tournament with teams from many countries. Soccer teams play in the World Cup every four years.

The players in the World Cup play for their country's team. They can also play for club teams.

INSIDE SOCCER

Lionel Messi plays for the club team Inter Miami CF and for Argentina's national team.

The first men's World Cup was in 1930. The first women's World Cup was in 1991. FIFA sets up the World Cups.

1991 women's World Cup

In the first men's World Cup, 13 teams played. The games were played in Uruguay. Uruguay's team won the tournament.

2022 Uruguay men's team

The Brazil men's national team has won the most World Cups. They have five wins.

The US women's national team has four. That's more than any other women's team!

INSIDE SOCCER

Some countries, including Canada, Mexico, and Scotland, have never won a World Cup.

More people watch the World Cup on TV than any other sports event. In 2022, more than one billion people watched the final game!

BRASIL
NEYMAR JR
10
BRASIL

Fans love the World Cup. People wear costumes in their team colors. They sing special chants for their country's team.

INSIDE SOCCER

"Olé! Olé! Olé!" is a popular World Cup chant.

After the World Cup, many countries celebrate. They have parades for their teams. Millions of people line the streets to see the players.

Coca-Cola
WELTMEISTER
WELTMEISTER. DAS SIND WIR ALLE!
Coca-Cola

Argentina won the men's World Cup in 2022. About four million fans joined the parade. The world celebrates soccer during the World Cup.

Glossary

celebrate: to do something special for a big event

FIFA: a group that runs pro soccer around the world

tournament: a series of games played to choose a champion

Learn More

Krenn, Cara. *Most Incredible Soccer Moments*. Minneapolis: Lerner Publications, 2026.

Leed, Percy. *Soccer: A First Look*. Minneapolis: Lerner Publications, 2023.

Simons, Lisa M. Bolt. *Curious About Soccer*. Mankato, MN: Amicus, 2024.

Index

fan, 18, 22

national, 9, 14

parade, 20, 22

player, 4, 8, 20

team, 6, 8–9, 12, 14, 18, 20

Photo Acknowledgments

Image credits: STAFF/Getty Images, p. 5; AP Photo/Richard Callis/SPP/Sipa USA, p. 7; AP Photo/Robert Michael/picture-alliance/dpa, p. 9; Bob Thomas/Getty Images, p. 11; AP Photo/The Yomiuri Shimbun, p. 13; AJ Johnson/ISI Photos/Getty Images, p. 15; AP Photo/Martin Mejia, p. 17; AP Photo/Robert Michael/picture-alliance/dpa, p. 19; AP Photo/Markus Gilliar/Pool, p. 21; Chris Brunskill/Fantasista/Getty Images, p. 23. Design elements: vid64/Getty Images; boytaro Thongbun/500px/Getty Images. Cover: AP Photo/Christophe Ena.